STONE ME

STONE ME

THE WIT AND WISDOM OF **KEITH RICHARDS**

COMPILED BY **MARK BLAKE**

 NEW AMERICAN LIBRARY

New American Library
Published by New American Library, a division of
Penguin Group (USA) Inc., 375 Hudson Street,
New York, New York 10014, USA
Penguin Group (Canada), 90 Eglinton Avenue East, Suite 700, Toronto,
Ontario M4P 2Y3, Canada (a division of Pearson Penguin Canada Inc.)
Penguin Books Ltd., 80 Strand, London WC2R 0RL, England
Penguin Ireland, 25 St. Stephen's Green, Dublin 2,
Ireland (a division of Penguin Books Ltd.)
Penguin Group (Australia), 250 Camberwell Road, Camberwell, Victoria 3124,
Australia (a division of Pearson Australia Group Pty. Ltd.)
Penguin Books India Pvt. Ltd., 11 Community Centre, Panchsheel Park,
New Delhi - 110 017, India
Penguin Group (NZ), 67 Apollo Drive, Rosedale, North Shore 0632,
New Zealand (a division of Pearson New Zealand Ltd.)
Penguin Books (South Africa) (Pty.) Ltd., 24 Sturdee Avenue,
Rosebank, Johannesburg 2196, South Africa

Penguin Books Ltd., Registered Offices:
80 Strand, London WC2R 0RL, England

Published by an imprint of New American Library, a division of Penguin Group (USA) Inc. This is an
authorized reprint of a hardcover edition published by Aurum Press Ltd. For information address Aurum
Press Ltd., 7 Greenland Street, London NW1 0ND.

First New American Library Printing, May 2009
10 9 8 7 6 5 4 3 2 1

CONTENTS

STONE ME

INTRODUCTION

No rock star's life is more shrouded in myth than that of Keith Richards. Tall tales abound: of near-death drug-induced comas; of cleansing blood transfusions; of marathon benders followed by a restorative shepherd's pie; of two functioning livers . . .

Then there are the stories from those who have encountered the man. One hapless Stones fan handed Keith a favorite guitar to autograph, only to watch as Keith drove off with it in his limo. After being flagged down at a traffic light, Richards simply growled through the window, "Buy another." Then there's the recording studio manager whose facility in the middle of the desert was equipped with panoramic windows onto the surrounding landscape. On arriving at the fabulously appointed room, the famously nocturnal guitarist could only mutter, "Cover that shit up."

One observer described Richards as "a monument to the mortician's art." His bandmate Ronnie Wood has long ventured the notion that only two life-forms would survive nuclear war: "Cockroaches—and Keith Richards." In his own words, Richards embraces the notion of "life as a wild animal," and his legendary close shaves have left him with a unique take on existence. Yet somehow, Keith Richards's implacably rock 'n' roll worldview has something to offer all of us . . .

KEITH'S EARLY DAYS

The legend of Keith Richards began in Dartford, Kent, on December 18, 1943. An only child growing up in the bomb sites of a postwar suburb, Keith discovered the guitar, rock 'n' roll, and a taste for mild delinquency. A chance encounter with a very old school friend Mick Jagger would prove fortuitous, and the two would eventually find their way to what became the Rolling Stones.

With pop stardom came the Keith

STONE ME

Richards persona: initially sullen and withdrawn; later the piratical lone ranger who would somehow dodge jail sentences and skirmishes with death and survive to tell the tale. Despite being the "Most Likely" on a list of "The Rock Stars Most Likely to Croak . . . ," Keith has outlasted ex-bandmates, ex–drug buddies and, so he claims, several of his own doctors. Yet as the man himself observes, "Every day of my life is show business." Start him up . . .

"I'm Sagittarius—half man, half horse with a license to shit in the street." 1984

On his date of birth
"Classic of '43. Don't knock it. A vintage year." 1988

On his upbringing
"I come from a weird mixture. Very stern on one side, and very frivolous, gay, artistic on the other." 1976

7

"I grew up in a council house. No phone, no TV, no car. We just did our own thing. You want to go somewhere? Get on the bike."

2003

"My grandfather was a saxophone player before he got gassed in World War 1 and couldn't blow anymore. My grandmother used to play piano with my grandfather until she caught him playing around with some other chick, and she refused to ever touch the piano again. I think she's even refused to fuck him since then." 1976

On discovering rock 'n' roll

"There was a certain point with my generation where something went *bang*! And suddenly rock 'n' roll came along. Little Richard, Elvis, Chuck Berry were all flying at me like an artillery barrage." 1997

On being a Boy Scout

"I was in the Beaver Patrol. Every year they had these huge jamborees. At one of them I smuggled in a couple of bottles of whiskey. Soon afterward a couple of fights went down between us and some Yorkshire guys. I went to slug one guy and hit the tent pole instead, and broke a bone in my hand." 1981

On his school days
"I used to wear two pairs of pants to school, a very tight pair and a very baggy pair, which I would just put on as soon as I got near the school, because they would send you home if you had tight pants on." **1978**

On learning to become a guitar hero
"I got the moves off first and I got the guitar later. A lot of it is watching yourself in your mum's wardrobe mirror, posing and getting the moves off." **1983**

"It becomes an obsession and sometimes it's an excuse. You're a shy boy. 'Shit, I'd rather sit here and play guitar than go out and make a fool of myself pulling chicks.'" 1983

On being an art student
"I went to art school and learned how to advertise, because you don't learn much art there. I schlepped my portfolio to one agency, and they said, 'Can you make a good cup of tea?' I said, 'Yeah, I can, but not for you.' I left my crap there and walked out." 2002

**On living in a shared house with
Mick Jagger and Brian Jones**
"There was mold growing on the walls and
nobody cleaning the joint up. We lived on
the second floor and on the ground floor
were these four students—chick teachers—
who got roped into doing the cleaning and
occasionally got knocked off
for their troubles." **1988**

On the early days of being in the Rolling Stones
"When we first started, we were looking at
that first record contract and thinking, 'Oh,
Christ! Two years at the most.' Nobody got
longer than that—except Elvis—and then you
were dead as a dodo." **2008**

"We certainly didn't want to be rock 'n' roll stars. That would be too tacky!" **1964**

"My mother never expected to see me on stage: 'He's such a shy boy!' She's been disabused of that." **2003**

On the early audience reaction to the Stones
"You took your life in your hands just to walk out there. It was all climbing over rooftops, getaways down fire escapes, through laundry chutes, into bakery vans. I was strangled twice." **2004**

"It was like the Battle of Crimea going on. People gasping, tits hanging out." **2004**

As one of a trio of boy sopranos ("There was me, Spike and Terry") in the choir at Dartford Technical School, Keith performed at London's Royal Festival Hall and also at Westminster Abbey, singing "Hallelujah" from Handel's Messiah, in front of the Queen ("My first taste of showbiz"). However, nature intervened after Richards turned thirteen. "When my voice broke at thirteen, the choirmaster said to me, 'You're the best soprano I've had in a long time, but it's gone now. Your career is over.'"

Encore!

"Rock 'n' roll's greatest
weapon is humor. If it
ain't fun, it's nothing."

1983

KEITH ON THE STONES

When Mick Jagger first announced his intention to make a solo album, Richards threatened to "cut his throat" if he toured with another band. Jagger did tour with another band, but lived to tell the tale. Richards, despite his own occasional solo ventures, has remained loyal to the sanctity of the Stones, proud and proprietorial to the present day. "We asked ourselves, 'Why are we doing this?' And the answer is 'We

have to,'" said Keith on the eve of the Stones'
1989 world tour. Twenty years later, they're
still doing it . . .

On the longevity of the Rolling Stones
"The future? I don't think about it. We all have visions of playing in our wheelchairs."
1969

"We're a determined group of lads. Nothing short of nuclear weapons is going to put this lot out of action." **1976**

"I read the other day that there was no reason why the Stones couldn't be like Sinatra or Bing Crosby, which I thought was an amazing comparison. In rock 'n' roll, nobody's ever done it." **1982**

19

"For younger generations born after 1963, '64, you've got the sun, the moon, the air they breathe, and you've got the Rolling Stones. We've always been there." **1985**

"The Stones move slowly . . . their wonders to perform. Did anybody moan at Beethoven [*sic*] for how long it took him to write the 1812 Overture?" **1986**

"People have this thing that we shouldn't be here: 'How dare they defy logic?' It's pure physical envy. They want to pull the rug out from under you, because they're bald and fat and can't move for shit." **2002**

On the relationships between the Stones
"These are cats you've probably spent more time with than your girlfriend or your family. Even though you didn't want to." **1986**

"Sometimes when you're in the dressing room before going on, you look around and think, There's Mick, there's Charlie, there's Ron? . . . All right? . . . There's me. And you suddenly think, Is that all there is? Where's the one that knows everything?" *1994*

"The Stones are such a weird chemical mixture of people, such an unlikely bunch. But
we're probably four of the most straight-up
guys you could actually meet." **1998**

On ex-Stones guitarist, the late Brian Jones
"I don't think honestly that you'll find anyone
who liked Brian. Brian was not a likable
guy. He had so many hang-ups he didn't
know where to hang himself . . . So he
drowned himself." **1988**

**Asked whether he thought Brian Jones
was murdered**

"No one will ever know . . .
Brian never told me." **1999**

On ex-Stones bassist Bill Wyman

"Bill Wyman's the most famous pisser of all
time. Once he starts he just can't stop. He's
a little bloke and I don't know where
he keeps the bladder but he just goes
on and on . . ." **1988**

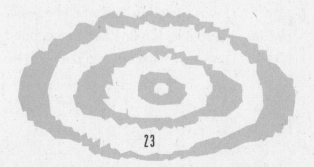

"Bill's from a different generation. For him, success is going on the Michael Aspel show. I think he's on his third menopause, certainly can't be his first." **1990**

"I could never understand Bill's thing about counting women. What are you gonna do with a chick in ten minutes, for Chrissake? It takes them half that long to get their drawers down." **1998**

"I did everything but hold him at gunpoint. I was pissed as hell when he went, because the rule is, No one leaves this band except in a coffin." **1992**

On guitarist Ronnie Wood

"Ronnie is a bigmouth. I love him dearly, but he's a flap-flap. I can never remember Ronnie pulling a gun on me. He wouldn't know which end to point." **2008**

"I've known him stoned out of his brain, and I've known him straight sober. Quite honestly, there's very little difference." **2002**

"Thank God for Ronnie Wood. They could be burying him and he'd still be laughing. The last thing you'd hear out of his coffin would be, 'Ahahahah!' " **1983**

"Ronnie was a piss artist. He never stopped. After the last tour, I stayed round his house and he'd wake up in the morning and go, 'Sambuca and water!' No, no, no, Ronnie, no." **2003**

On drummer Charlie Watts

"Charlie hates going on the road. He only ever carries a hold-all with a change of clothes in it, because he likes to pretend he's going home the next day." **1979**

"How can you describe a guy who buys a 1936 Alfa Romeo just to look at the dashboard? Charlie can't drive." **2005**

"If there's something between Mick and I, it's Charlie I've got to talk to. I'll say, 'Charlie, should I go to Mick's room and hang him?'" **2002**

"Charlie always says he doesn't want to go on tour, but he always does. Charlie's one of those guys who appear over the poop deck after it's all over and says, 'I quite enjoyed that.'" **1981**

"I don't want to butter the man up, but he really is the best fucking drummer. He should be Prime Minister." **2005**

Keith is known to have physically attacked at least two of his band members. Just before going onstage in Catford, South London, in the early '60s, Richards blacked Brian Jones's eye after the guitarist ate a piece of Richards's preshow chicken dinner without his permission ("Have you eaten it, you cunt?" . . . Whack! . . . "Ladies and gentlemen, the Rolling Stones!"). His most public display of displeasure came at Wembley Stadium on the band's 1982 tour. When Richards fluffed the riff to "She's So Cold," he looked round, expecting Ronnie Wood to cover him. Seeing Wood looking less than compos mentis, Keith punched him in the face for not paying attention— receiving a round of applause from the audience.

Encore!

"You do, occasionally,
just look at your feet and
think, 'This is the same
old shit every night.'"

1997

KEITH ON WOMEN AND GUITARS

"The shape of the guitar is really feminine," claims Keith. "There's many times I've slept with that fucker." Though he's been married to former model Patti Hansen since 1983, his passion for the instrument of his trade has been the most enduring love affair of his life. While he's been overshadowed by the sexual antics of his lead singer, Richards's approach to women, sex and romance casts him as both an unreconstructed rocker and an old-school gentleman. But, ultimately, it all comes back to that plank of wood . . .

On his earliest pinups
"I'm very keen on Sophia Loren. There, as they say, *is* a bird." 1964

"If I was suddenly stuck alone, I could stop myself going mad as long as I suddenly had a guitar." 1989

After being criticized for the lyric "Black girls just wanna get fucked all night" in the Stones song "Some Girls"
"We write our songs from personal experience. OK, so over the years we happened to meet extra-horny black chicks." 1978

On groupies

"We actually used to look on groupies as
gas stations. Uh . . . we're in Cincinnati . . .
We need to fill her up." **2008**

"The thing about groupies is, it wasn't just
boinky-boinky. They used to take care of
you. They used to rub Vicks on your chest if
you had a cold." **2008**

On sharing women with Jagger

"All the chicks liked me better than Mick."

1989

"I've stolen quite a few chicks off him and he's nudged his way into my lot, but not significantly." 2006

When asked the standard interview question: What do you want to do next?
"Britney Spears." 2004

On love and romance
"Chicks see the other side of me, which guys don't. I have a good empathy with women. Nobody ever divorced *me*." 2002

"Chicks are always an education. I can have a load more fun with chicks than with a bunch of guys. One of the things I like to do is listen to chicks talk. What are they on about? What are they saying about us? A lot of good songs can come out of that." **1992**

"You know, there's nothing more disturbing than two chicks whispering to each other." 1978

"I've never just been interested in a lay. I've never started a relationship just for the purpose of wham-bam-thank-you-ma'am. Chicks are too precious for that. I love them too much to just roll over and stick it in." **1984**

On his marriage to Patti Hansen
"Shit, I'm gonna try anything. And if I'm gonna try anything like marriage, I'm gonna try it once. I ain't letting that bitch go." **1983**

When asked which model of guitar he likes best
"Give me five minutes and I'll make 'em all sound the same." **1986**

**The Stones' women have all faced
the challenge of infiltrating their
notorious boys' club. None more so
than Ron Wood's future wife, Jo. On
their first "date," Woody arrived
unexpectedly at Jo's Paris hotel at
4:30 a.m., with Keith in tow. To Jo's
astonishment, Richards stayed with
the couple in the tiny room, taking
drugs for three days, before remembering that he actually had a flat
nearby that they should all move to,
as it had "much more space."**

*

Encore!

"Ask any of my women—
I'm really just attached
to this wooden stick." 2005

KEITH VS. MICK

"**M**ost lead vocalists aren't musicians—they're fairies," declared Keith in 1976. Elaborating on the fundamental difference between himself and the Rolling Stones' lead singer, Richards later said, "Mick Jagger has to dictate to life. To me, life's a wild animal." Theirs is a relationship as mercurial and complex as any marriage, with Richards rarely shy about *teasing, slagging and, occasionally, praising his childhood friend, musical foil, business partner, surrogate "wife" and the man he once nicknamed "Brenda." "I insult him," reflected Keith, "but he has the hide of a rhino . . ."*

On their conflicting approaches to life
"Mick drunk? . . . Oh, man, that's a sight to behold." **1982**

"In the '70s I was devoting much of my time to scoring and taking dope. Mick had to cover for me. That cat worked his butt off. He covered my ass. I owe Mick." **1985**

"Until the beginning of the '80s, you could have called me up in the North Pole and Mick in the South Pole and we would have said the same thing: I didn't change. He did." **1987**

"I've known Mick since I was four years old, and despite myself I do love the guy. But if you're Mick Jagger you should be a little less hung up about being Mick Jagger." 1988

"Ninety-nine percent of the male population would give a limb to live the way Mick Jagger does. To be Mick Jagger. And he's not happy." 1989

"I think he takes everything too seriously. My aim is always to try and introduce a bit of levity into his life." **1999**

"We kinda orbit around each other until we end up colliding." 2004

"Mick never drinks anything except soda water now. There's a closet queen, y'know."

2006

On Jagger, the surrogate wife

"Mick and I can never get divorced. We'd still have to look after the kids." **1989**

"Who's the wife? That's what you want to know. Who's the bitch? He's a good bitch. He's a good old girl." **2005**

"We're a Mom-and-Pop operation . . . He's Mom. I'm Pop." **2005**

On Jagger's legendary sexual prowess
"Mick talks all the time. He probably talks
when he's on the job." **1989**

*"Oh, his cock's on the end of his
nose, and a very small one at that.
Huge balls. Small cock.
Ask Marianne Faithfull."* **2005**

✳

On Mick's tangled love life
"I'm always sorry for Mick's women, because they end up crying on my shoulder. And I'm like, 'How do you think I feel? I'm *stuck* with him.'" **2003**

To a group of journalists backstage on the Stones' 1982 tour, after hearing how Jagger had slighted a member of their support band
"That's a fair example of the kind of cunt I've had to deal with for the last twenty-five years."

On the sexual chemistry between Mick and Keith
"We've never had sex with each other. I never fancied bum. At least not male bum. I may have accidentally slipped into a couple of females. Second hole down from the back of the neck, son—that's the one you want."

1994

"I don't fancy him. Otherwise he'd be fair game. But even in the most desperate situation . . . I'd rather fuck a puddle." **1999**

"In the '70s Jagger was camp. A
load of excruciating painful
campness went on. But I have no
idea if anyone ever shoved
it up the shitter." 2008

Discussing Jagger's 2002 solo album, *Goddess in the Doorway*, renamed by Keith "Dogshit in the Doorway"

"I listened to three tracks and gave up on it. Wimpy songs, wimpy performances, bad recording."

On Sir Michael Jagger

"I said to Mick, 'It's a fucking paltry honor.' If you're into this shit, hang on for the peerage. I don't want to step out onstage with someone wearing a fucking coronet and sporting the old ermine. I wouldn't let any member of the Royal Family near me with a sword." **2004**

In 1980 Jagger's latest squeeze—and future wife—Jerry Hall informed an interviewer that "Mick is the sexiest man in the world and the best lover I've ever had . . . I can't believe how weird and dirty he is." Richards took great pleasure in having the interview cutting taped to the side of his amp during rehearsals for the Stones' 1982 tour.

Encore!

"Occasionally you want to
strangle even the closest
of friends." 1997

KEITH VS. THE LAW

"We're in danger of becoming respectable," moaned Keith in 1966. A year later, he was sentenced to a stint in prison—swiftly curtailed—for possession of drugs. Eleven years later, Richards was busted for possession in Toronto. Despite expectations ("The rest of the band were very ticked off I didn't get put away for

*thirty years"), Keith escaped a jail sentence
and has remained a free man ever since.
Nevertheless, a penchant for firearms and
knives for, so he claims, "self-defense and
aesthetic reasons" has preserved a veneer of
lawlessness that Keith seems in no hurry to
dismiss . . .*

On getting busted in January 1967
"The level of drug education at Sussex CID
was minimal. They left a bag of heroin down
the sofa but took the incense sticks . . . I
said to one of the women they brought with
them to search the ladies, 'Would you mind
stepping off that Moroccan cushion because
you're ruining the tapestries?'" **1985**

Recalling his 1967 court appearance
"When I wasn't high I was in court. You try
saying 'Guilty, Your Honor' twenty-five
times in Marlborough Street and keep a
straight face." **1986**

STONE ME

**On the '60s establishment's attitude toward the
Rolling Stones**

"A country that's been running a thousand
years worried about two herberts running
around? Do me a favor. That's when you
realize how fragile our little society is. But
the government allowed that fragility to
show. They let us look under their skirts—
Oooh, just another pussy." **1995**

After being released from prison in July 1967
"Neither the accommodations nor the fashion suited me at all. I like a little more room. I like the john to be in a separate area, and I hate to be woken up. The food's awful, the wine list is terrible and the library is abysmal." **1985**

Discussing his weapons of choice
"You're never alone with a Smith and Wesson." **1973**

"I carry my trusty blade, and on the road I carry a .38 Special revolver. The .38's for business . . . I haven't actually used it in years, but I shoot hats with it just to make sure it works." **1999**

After being arrested in his hotel room by the Canadian police in 1977
"What disappointed me was that none of them was wearing a proper Mounties uniform. They were all in anoraks with droopy moustaches and bald heads. I'd have woken up a lot quicker if I'd seen the red tunic and Smokey Bear hat." **1977**

"I just wish they'd pick on the Sex Pistols. I've done my stint in the dock." 1977

After accidentally shooting Ronnie Wood's pet budgerigar in 1979
"Nobody told me it was a fucking real budgerigar."

STONE ME

After hitting a stage invader with his guitar in 1982

"What if he had a fuckin' gun in his hand or a knife? I mean, he might be a fan, he might be a nutter, and he's on my turf. I'm gonna chop the mother down!"

Keith's attitude to the law is exemplified by his attitude toward cars and driving. Richards failed his first driving test in 1965, but seemed to have acquired a license two years later. By then, he'd purchased a Bentley S Touring Continental, which he nicknamed "The Blue Lena," after jazz singer Lena Horne. As well as having a record player installed, Keith decorated the car with Turkish embassy flags, to give the impression that it was a diplomatic vehicle and avoid being stopped by the police.

In 1975, Richards overturned his latest set of wheels, "The Pink Lena," *in a field alongside the M1 just outside Newport Pagnell. The police apprehended him wandering along the motorway's hard shoulder, wearing sunglasses. It was four a.m. When an unidentified substance was found in his possession, Richards was arrested. He arrived two hours late for the subsequent trial, informing the court that he had been waiting for his trousers to be returned from the dry cleaner. "I find it extraordinary," said the judge, "that a man of your stature has only one pair of trousers."*

Encore!

"In the old days, customs officers used to go through me with a fine-tooth comb. Nowadays it's 'Oh, it's Keith. He's not a real problem. Whatever he's got, he probably forgot it anyway.' " 2003

KEITH ON MUSIC

Keith Richards's earliest musical colleagues recall a man hung up on simplicity, authenticity and honesty in music, recoiling from unnecessary virtuosity to such an extreme that he once dubbed the Shadows "wanky" on account of their nifty guitar work. A disciple of blues, soul and country, Richards has survived numerous musical trends, be it punk in the '70s ("Keith was the first punk. You can't outpunk Keith," said Mick Jagger), electronic pop in the '80s ("They forgot how to play and just pushed buttons. Give me a drum beat.") and countless imitators in the '90s ("The Black Crowes? . . . Are those the cats that want to be me?").

On songwriting

"There's only one song, and Adam and Eve wrote it; the rest is a variation on a theme."

1997

On Chuck Berry

"I've tried being a great guitar player and, like Chuck Berry, I have failed." **1975**

"I wouldn't warm to Chuck Berry if he was cremated next to me." **1979**

On the Beatles

"The Beatles were a great enema. That makes us a great toilet bowl." **2008**

On the Stones' imitators

"I only listen to black music these days. I ain't too interested in white bands who rip off white bands who ripped off black bands." **1976**

Discussing "hot new band" Led Zeppelin in *NME*

"I played their album quite a few times when I first got it, but then the guy's voice started to get on my nerves." **1969**

**On Zeppelin's singer Robert Plant and drummer
John Bonham**
"A couple of clueless Ernies from the
Midlands." **1975**

**On being asked what he thought about Led
Zeppelin's front-page-news reunion in 2007**
"They had one? . . . Fuck off." **2008**

On punk rock
"What's that band who sound like the
Doors? . . . The Stranglers? . . . I hate them."
1979

STONE ME

On Rod Stewart

"I listened to that single Rod put out ["Do Ya Think I'm Sexy?"] and I look at the peroxide hair, and I like the guy—I always have done—but I feel like saying, 'Now look, cunt, you don't need it.'" **1979**

On Boy George

"Ronnie [Wood] fancied him. Ronnie's in New York watching MTV and he drags me up and goes, 'You gotta see this chick, man.' I was already hip to it. 'Her name's George, Ron.'" **1982**

Remembering an encounter with Duran Duran during the recording of the Stones' 1986 album, *Dirty Work*

"You get Duran Duran coming down for a day, and saying, 'What are you doing in that room together?' It's called playing music, man. It's the only way we record— you snotty little turd." **1998**

*

On Bruce Springsteen

"I like Bruce. He's a good fucking journeyman, y'know. But he's holding the fort until something better comes along. If there was anything better around, he'd still be working the bars of New Jersey." **1986**

STONE ME

On Prince

"I've never liked Prince. Everybody else does and thinks I'm an arsehole for not liking him. But I think he's an overrated midget." 1988

On Michael Jackson

"Michael has a fantastic voice but I don't know why he keeps cutting his face up and indulging in these ludicrous personal hang-ups. Having your face chopped up like that can only mean he doesn't like himself." 1988

On heavy metal

"It's supposed to be heavy, but it's not supposed to just thunder down some endless runway like a plane that never takes off. I don't know where Metallica's inspiration comes from, but if it's me, then I fucked up." 1993

"If you want heavy metal, talk to John Lee Hooker—listen to that motherfucker play. That's heavy metal. That's armor!" 1993

On the Stones' classic, "Satisfaction"

"I always thought it was album filler. It could just as well have been called 'Aunt Millie's Caught Her Tit in the Mangle'" 2004

STONE ME

**On his feud with Elton John, during which Keith
took to calling Elton by his real name, Reg,
and "Reg" described Richards as resembling
"a monkey with arthritis"**
"All I said was I thought 'Candle in the
Wind' was a bit tacky, and said, 'Songs for
dead blondes.' I'd find it difficult to ride on
the back of that, but Reg is showbiz.
Oh, man, what an old bitch." **1999**

Discussing Oasis singer Liam Gallagher's challenge to Mick Jagger and Paul McCartney

"I'd like to have seen Liam Gallagher take on Mick and Paul. It didn't rile me. I thought it was funny. My attitude was, Come back when you grow up. Having said that, we've all done it. I threw out a challenge to Billy Fury forty years ago." **2004**

On David Bowie

"Who's David Bowie? Oh, he went to the same art school as me. Not a large fan, no. It's all pose. It's all fucking posing." **2008**

After receiving a congratulatory phone call from jazz bandleader Hoagy Carmichael
"Fuck me! That was like taking a call from Beethoven." 1978

Though an unlikely musical alliance, Keith Richards once shared a studio shift with electro-pop pioneers Ultravox. It was 1976 and Ultravox were recording their debut album during the day, while Richards spent the night overseeing mixes for what would become the Stones' Love You Live album. On their first morning in the studio, Ultravox and tape op-

erator Steve Lillywhite encountered Richards passed out in a chair in front of the console. Unable to wake him, Lillywhite put on a tape of the band's latest drum track, cranked up the volume and stood back. Despite the din, Richards remained immobile, except for one foot, which suddenly started keeping time. Eventually, the band wheeled the chair containing a still-slumbering Keith into the corridor. An hour later, he came round, unfazed by his new surroundings, and poked his head back into the studio for a friendly chat before whizzing home in his Bentley.

Encore!

"Me? I just want to be
Muddy Waters. Even though
I'll never be that good or
that black." 1997

KEITH VS. THE HUMAN BODY

T he jokes began around the middle of the 1970s, when Keith's rare appearances in public fueled the rumors that he was not long for this world. Physically cadaverous and sometimes mentally disorientated, he seemed to be doing a grand impression of the living dead. But that was then. His brain cells and internal organs may have taken an extraordinary battering, but Keith is still here. Still functioning. How

*does he manage it? "I eat everything wrong.
I shove terrible things inside me," he admits.
"But doctors want to study my body after I
die, and figure out how to make other people
much better . . ."*

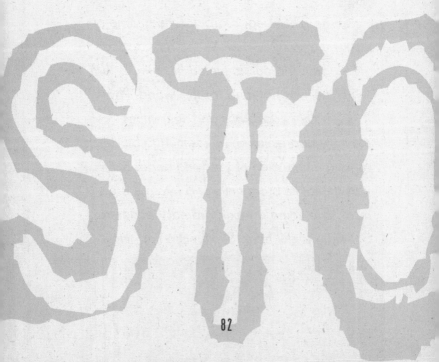

On having a pretour medical
"The doctor stuck electrodes all over my body, hooked up more monitors than the Stones use onstage, and told me I was 'normal.' Fuck! Can you imagine telling Keith Richards he's 'normal.'" **1994**

"People's perceptions change radically when you croak." **1994**

"I've had about three doctors who've told me, 'If you carry on like this, you will be dead in six months.' I went to *their* funerals."

2007

"I do have an incredible immune system. I had hepatitis C—and cured it by myself. Just by being me." **2008**

"Doing a Rolling Stones show for two hours a night, that's enough fuckin' exercise, you know? Then I've got to go to bed with the old lady . . . bonka-bonka." **2008**

On his disappearing—and then reappearing—teeth
"You've only got to have one broken tooth for everyone to think you're a villain. There was a point where I could groove on it, but another chunk fell off and since then it's fallen out of favor with me." **1974**

"Miraculously, due to abstinence and prayer, my teeth grew back." 1979

After falling out of a tree on holiday and sustaining brain damage in 2006
"Fiji is the worst place in the world to have brain damage." 2008

"I said to the anaesthetist, 'Listen, it's pretty hard to put me out.'" 2008

"I feel no different except I've got six titanium pins in my head. They went in there—they had a look. The doctor had turned gray by the time I woke up." 2006

On staying up for nine nights in a row
"You lose track after three days. An hour becomes a minute. A minute becomes an hour. Everything becomes a beautiful blur . . . until you fall over and break your nose." 2004

On recuperating after a tour

"I hunker down in my decompression chamber with my mates and my wife and my grandkids, and I lie there and they feed me." **2008**

"The best thing to do is to go off to a totally different place, preferably a very warm beach with a good bitch." **2003**

On his unusual dietary habits

"HP Sauce is harder to kick than heroin."

1986

"I've got a connection here in New York for HP Sauce. There's a guy from Yorkshire has got a store downtown here, and you can get everything: steak and kidney pies, puddings, custard, the lot . . ." **1988**

"Cheese is very wrong. Fermented milk is not the ideal choice for everyday eating. Cheese don't make it." **1996**

On reaching a ripe old age
"When I was younger, I said, 'If I live to thirty I'll shoot myself.' You reach thirty and put the gun away." **2007**

"I'm sixty, am I? . . . I knew it was one of
those with a zero on the end.
Sixty? . . . Christ!" 2004

**In 1998, the Stones were forced to
postpone dates on their Bridges to
Babylon tour, when Richards sustained
three broken ribs and a punctured
lung after a fall from a ladder at
his home in Connecticut. Earlier, the
Guggenheim Museum in Manhat-
tan had contacted the guitarist and
asked him to draw a human figure,
with a view to selling the sketch at**

a charity auction. "I thought, 'Well, if I'm going to do this, I'll check with the master,'" recalled Keith. Late one night, he decided to retrieve his copy of Leonardo da Vinci's Treatise on Anatomy from the top shelf of his library. "It's about eighteen feet up. As I touched the top shelf the whole fucking thing just came down on me. Blitzed me. So you've got to say that I did learn quite a bit about anatomy. That Leonardo, man. He's a rough teacher."

Encore!

"I was Number 1 on the 'Who's Likely to Die' list for ten years. I was really disappointed when I fell off." 1997

KEITH ON EXCESS

"We're not boozers, but we enjoy a drink and a fag like anybody else," Richards told the press in 1964, with little indication of the bedlam to come. By the '70s, Keith was the most famous drug user on the planet, held up as a cautionary tale by parents, teachers and law enforcement officers the world over. Clawing his way back to some semblance of normality in recent years, the guitarist has become a rueful, honest and sometimes unapologetic commentator on his perils of substance abuse. "I took drugs because I wanted to hide," he once admitted. "Life was just too bloody public and that was the only place where I could handle it and be in my own cocoon."

On why he started taking drugs

"It's a matter of making the next gig. Like the bomber pilots—if you've got to bomb Dresden tomorrow, you get yourself four or five bennies to make the trip and keep yourself together . . . Here, Squadron Leader, open your mouth and I'll pop a couple of these blighters in." **1988**

On that excessive reputation

"My father said to me, 'Keith, there's a difference between scratching your arse and tearing it to bits.' I've always borne that in mind." **1996**

"I've been drunk for twenty-seven years." **1980**

"I've never had problems with drugs. Only with policemen." **1988**

"I've studied this shit. I'm a walking laboratory. I'm Baudelaire rolled in with a few other cats." **1997**

"I never went in for these fancy-named drugs. Ecstasy? Anything with a name like that I wouldn't touch. I went for the basics." **1988**

"I'm polytoxic. But I will write all your epitaphs." 2002

"I don't do as much as everybody thinks but I probably do more than they imagine. I don't encourage anyone to do what I do . . . Everybody's a hypochondriac. Except me . . . I've got everything else." 2006

On taking heroin

"I must say, in all fairness to the poppy, that never once did I have a cold. The cure to the common cold is there—but, of course, they daren't let anybody know because you'd have a nation full of dope addicts." 1979

97

STONE ME

"I don't know if I've been extremely lucky or if it's that subconscious careful, but I've never turned blue in someone else's bathroom. I consider that the height of bad manners."
1980

"I wouldn't do anything with needles these days. You ain't gonna inject talent into yourself." **1992**

"A nice fix at breakfast, one for elevenses and another one at teatime. It was like breaks at the cricket or something." **2005**

"I was always a very active junkie. Wouldn't dream of going up and skiing without a good shot." 2007

"I'm a fucking superstar, but when I want the stuff, baby, I'm down on the ground with the rest of them." 2008

On trying to abstain
"After ten years of trying to kill myself, I decided I better get on with my life." 1979

On excess in the 21st Century

"The wife's always asking, 'Why are you lighting up another cigarette?' I tell her it's because the last one wasn't long enough."

2002

"I occasionally borrow pot from my kids. They do a little weed occasionally. 'Here, Dad.' Or more likely, 'Dad, have you got any?'" **2008**

"There was a knock on our dressing room door. Our manager shouted, 'Keith! Ron! The Police are here!' Oh, man, we panicked, flushed everything down the john. Then the door opened and it was Stewart Copeland and Sting." 1982

On supposedly snorting his dad's ashes
"The strangest thing I've tried to snort? My father, I snorted my father. He was cremated and I couldn't resist grinding him up with a little bit of blow. My dad wouldn't have cared. It went down pretty well and I'm still alive." 2007

STONE ME

Commenting on the story that he'd snorted his dad's ashes
"I said I'd chopped him up *like* cocaine, not *with*. I opened his box up and . . . out comes a bit of dad on the dining room table. I'm going, 'I can't use a brush and dustpan for this.'" **2007**

Keith's most enduring legend concerns his so-called "blood change." A throwaway remark to reporters in 1973 led to the story that in order to cleanse his body of heroin, Richards was checking into a clinic in Switzerland and submitting to a transfusion in which his own blood would be replaced by a clean supply. A year later Keith was poking fun at the story ("I'd like to have it done, because eating motorway food for ten years has done my blood no good at all"). Nevertheless, the story still spread, adding to the notion of Richards's indestructibility and giving rise to fantastic speculation that he was somehow possessed of vampiric powers (another theory at the time was that he had two livers). "I wouldn't change this blood for anything, man, because I might get somebody else's and not be the same," he admitted years later. "Although I've no doubt my blood would say, 'You stupid cunt, you've changed me quite a lot.'"

Encore!

"Some people still think I'm a junkie who lives in a coffin. I'm really just a benign old chap." 1994

KEITH'S PHILOSOPHY OF LIFE

I n court on drug charges in 1967, Keith Richards's QC asked him, "What has success meant to you?" to which the guitarist replied, "A complete lack of privacy since 1963." Nowadays, Keith expresses the mixed sentiments of a World War II baby, unreconstructed rock star and traditional British male, delivering his bons mots with all the timing of an accomplished after-dinner speaker. "What's the biggest lesson life has taught me?" he pondered in 2007. "Keep breathing."

On music, career and ambition

"Everything I've ever planned has never worked out. I've relied on accidents all my life." **2001**

"I've said it before: this is all I can do. I'm a lousy plumber." **1989**

"I love my kids most of the time, and I love my wife most of the time. Music I love all the time." **1988**

"The idea of retiring is like killing yourself. It's almost like hari-kari. I intend to live to be one hundred and go down in history." **2004**

"I've seen murders. I've seen dogs come onstage, trying to savage people. I've turned around and found a pool of blood where the piano player should be! But you can't really do anything about that—it's just part of the gig." **2003**

"Music's always been streaks ahead of any other gig. After air, food, water and fucking, I think music is the next human necessity."

1983

"I've always felt totally blessed. I've never said 'Yes, sir' since I left school and people have paid me to do it." **2005**

"The greatest epitaph a musician can have is: 'RIP, he passed it on.'"

1983

On self-doubt

"I've never had inner turmoil about all this. You find a lot of people these days who cannot stand to be alone. You could lock me up in solitary for weeks on end, and I'd keep myself amused." **2008**

"There's a thin line between vulnerable and asshole." 1992

Asked what it was like watching his house burn down in 1968

"It's not the most pleasant experience—sitting in your joint and the fucker combusts."

On politics

"How can you worry about world population? Whose problem is that? You tell me. I mean, what about that tidal wave in Pakistan, man? Quarter of a million in one night. I'll just keep on rocking and hope for the best." 1971

On race

"I love Paris, hate the people. Paris would be lovely without the Parisians." **1978**

"I like hanging with black people. They think I am one anyway. I'm just in disguise. To me, the other side of the tracks is where I can really rest." **1997**

"It doesn't matter where you were born or who you think you are . . . You're fucking African." **2000**

"Basically, I'm Jamaican . . . Yeah, mon! Lion! . . . Bloodclaat, mon!"

1983

Taking exception to the Stones' increasingly elaborate stage shows

"I absolutely draw the line at elephants. Even with trousers on." **1976**

On technology and the 21st century

"I've always looked on the computer as like . . . Well, now *everybody* wants to be a fucking typist." **2006**

"Synthesisers and the Internet are things that really should have been kept secret." **2005**

"I don't personally have a computer . . . A mouse? I put the cat on it." **2002**

On his plans for the new millennium

"I'm going to go back into the bunker and see if this next millennium actually happens. I've got a few machine guns, a stash of cash, some tinned food . . . and I'm waiting. I don't want to know until at least January 31." **1999**

**Asked what advice he would have given his
younger self**
"Do exactly what you're doing. You'll end up
like me, and don't worry about it." **2006**

"Don't do that again!" 2003

Keith has long enthused on the joys of family life, while acknowledging the more unconventional aspects of his children's upbringing. As a boy, his eldest son, Marlon, was a fixture on Stones tours during the wild '70s. "My upbringing compared to his was very mundane," conceded Keith. "Mine was a cap and satchel. Whereas he was buzzing around in a Bentley, waking his dad up with a broom because, you know, he's got a shooter under the pillow." Keith's daughter Dandelion changed her name by deed poll to Angela as soon as she could legally do so, informing her father that "she'd kill me if I ever called her Dandelion again." Marriage to Patti Hansen brought daughters Theodora and Alexandra ("I was expecting to be a grandfather before I got to be a father again," admitted Keith in 1986. "But you roll over in the middle of the night, and, boy, there you go"). Now Richards has assumed the role of the doting granddad: "Watching kids grow is the greatest pleasure. Though grandkids are an even better thing, because you can hand them back."

Encore!

"I'm all for a quiet life.
I just didn't get one." 2006